Dessert Designer

CREATING AMAZING CUPCAKES

WHAT'S UP, CUPCAKE?

by Dana Meachen Rau

CAPSTONE PRESS
a capstone imprint

Snap Books are published by Capstone Press,
1710 Roe Crest Drive, North Mankato, Minnesota 56003.
www.capstonepub.com

Library of Congress Cataloging-in-Publication Data
Rau, Dana Meachen, 1971–
 What's up, cupcake?: creating amazing cupcakes / by Dana
Meachen Rau.
 p. cm.—(Snap books. Dessert designer)
 Includes bibliographical references and index.
 Summary: "Step-by-step instructions teach readers how to create
food art with cupcakes"—Provided by publisher.
 ISBN 978-1-4296-8617-4 (library binding)
 ISBN 978-1-62065-340-1 (ebook pdf)
 1. Cupcakes—Juvenile literature. I. Title.
TX771.R387 2013
641.8'653—dc23   2011051564

Editor: Jennifer Besel
Designer: Juliette Peters
Food and Photo Stylist: Brent Bentrott
Prop Preparation: Sarah Schuette
Scheduler: Marcy Morin
Production Specialist: Kathy McColley

Photo Credits:
All photos by Capstone Studio/Karon
Dubke except:
Tania McNaboe, p. 32 (author's photo)

Printed in the United States of America in
North Mankato, Minnesota.
072016   009898R

Table of Contents

Introduction

Projects

Extras

A PIECE OF CAKE!

Puppies, kittens, and babies—everything is cuter when it's small. The same is true for desserts. Cupcakes are mini-sized cakes. Sure, they're cute, but there are other reasons to make cupcakes too.

- **CUPCAKES ARE FAST FOOD.**
They cook faster than a big cake.

- **CUPCAKES END ARGUMENTS.**
All servings are the same size, so no one fights for the biggest slice.

- **CUPCAKES KEEP YOU BUSY.**
Need something to do on a rainy day? Get decorating!

- **CUPCAKES ARE CREATIVE.**
Discover your inner artist. A cupcake may be small, but it has plenty of room for your big ideas.

There are no rules when it comes to cupcake creations. For the cake, use any flavor you like. Make your own or buy unfrosted cupcakes from a bakery. Cover your cupcakes with frosting like an artist covers a canvas. Add layers of color with candy and cookies. With a little imagination, your cupcakes will be little works of art.

How to Use This Book

Ready to get started? It's a piece of cake! Start by gathering the supplies you need. You may already have the ingredients in your kitchen. But if not, all the supplies can be found in grocery stores or the cake-decorating aisles of craft and hobby stores.

Then follow the simple steps for each project to create your cute cupcakes. Remember to always ask for an adult's help if you are using a knife, microwave, or other kitchen appliance.

~ Fluffy Frosting ~

Some dessert fans insist that the frosting is the best part of a cupcake. This sweet goo also helps hold your creations together. Store-bought frosting tastes great and is easy to spread and pipe onto your cupcake. But if you're eager to tie on an apron and make frosting from scratch, here's a simple recipe. It makes about 2½ cups (600 milliliters) of frosting.

Ingredients
½ cup (120 mL) unsalted butter, softened to room temperature
½ teaspoon (2.5 mL) vanilla extract
2 cups (480 mL) confectioners' sugar
1–2 tablespoons (15–30 mL) milk

Tools
large bowl
measuring cups and spoons
electric hand mixer
spatula

Steps
1. In a large bowl, cream the butter and vanilla with the mixer on medium speed until fluffy.
2. Beating on low, alternate adding sugar and milk until the ingredients are mixed well. The frosting should be thick, creamy, and spreadable. Scrape the sides of the bowl often with the spatula.
3. Store the frosting in the refrigerator in an airtight container. Bring it to room temperature and rewhip before using.

For chocolate frosting, follow the recipe above, and add ¼ cup (60 mL) unsweetened cocoa powder along with the sugar.

DECORATOR'S TOOLBOX

A painter needs brushes and canvases. A carpenter needs hammers and nails. A cupcake decorator like you needs tools too!

~ wax paper ~
Use this supply to keep taffy and other sticky stuff from sticking to your workspace.

~ decorating tips ~
These go on the piping bag to create cool designs with frosting.

~ piping bag ~
This fabric or plastic bag holds frosting and is used to decorate cakes and cupcakes.

~ tweezers ~
Use tweezers to place those tiny decorations in just the right place.

~ cutting board ~
Do any cutting on the cutting board to avoid damaging kitchen counters.

~ toothpicks and wooden skewers ~
These are great for helping keep layers together or to stick decorations to a project.

~ bowls ~
Keep a variety of these around to mix up frosting. Make sure that bowls used for melting candy are microwave safe.

~ kitchen shears ~
These scissors are designed for use with food.

~ cooling rack ~
Not only is this tool good for cooling goodies, but the slats let frosting drip off a project for a smooth finish.

~ rolling pin ~
This is a handy tool for flattening taffies or crushing candies.

~ food coloring ~
Food coloring makes your frosting stand out. Just put a drop of liquid or a dab of gel into your frosting. You'll find a little goes a long way.

~ sharp knife ~
You need this to score candy or cut cupcakes.

~ spreader ~
This might be the most handy decorating tool. Use it to cover a surface with a smooth layer of frosting.

~ zip-top bags ~
These make a great substitute for piping bags.

~ fork ~
This isn't just for eating with! Use a fork to pick cupcakes up to make them easier to frost.

~ spoons ~
Have a bunch of spoons ready to stir up a rainbow of frosting colors.

ALOHA LEI CUPCAKES

A Hawaiian luau is the ultimate beach bash. Tropical parties
need necklaces of flowers—especially ones you can eat!
Enjoy these tasty blooms, then hula until sunset.

INGREDIENTS
vanilla frosting
12 mini cupcakes
36 jellybeans
96 wafer candies
   in a variety of colors
18 green wafer candies

1. Frost the top of each cupcake.

2. Place three jellybeans in the center of each cupcake. Surround the jellybeans with four wafer candy petals. Then add four more petals behind the first ones.

3. With an adult's help, gently drag a knife across the surfaces of the green wafers to score them. Don't try to cut straight through the wafers or they will crack.

4. Break the green wafers in half along the scored line.

5. Tuck the green wafer pieces behind the petals to look like leaves.

6. Arrange the cupcakes on a platter to look like a lei.

Makes 12 flower cupcakes

~ A Basket of Blooms ~
You can also arrange these flower cupcakes in a basket. Cut a block of flower foam to fit tightly in a basket. Cover the foam with plastic wrap. Poke a lollipop stick into the foam. Place a cupcake on the stick to hold it in place. Repeat with more lollipop sticks and cupcakes until you have a bunch of beautiful blooms.

BERRY BASKET

A tisket, a tasket, a tasty cupcake basket. Serve up these cupcakes for a *berry* amazing treat!

INGREDIENTS

vanilla frosting
1 mini cupcake
    (paper liner removed)
1 graham cracker square
8 vanilla or chocolate cream
    wafer cookies
1 orange or brown licorice twist
raspberries, blackberries,
    or blueberries

1. Frost the top of the cupcake. Also spread some frosting on the bottom of the cupcake. Set the cupcake on the graham cracker to make a base.

2. Spread frosting on one wide side of each wafer cookie. Stack the cookies around the cupcake like a basket. If needed, add frosting to the edges to help them stick to the cupcake and base.

3. Arch the licorice twist and tuck it into opposite corners of the basket.

4. Place the berries on top of the cupcake so it looks like a full basket.

5. For a special touch, add a ribbon to the handle.

Makes 1 basket

~ sweets in All seasons ~

When berries are out of season, look for raspberry and blackberry candies. They'll give you a taste of summer any time of year!

FLUFFY BUNNY

Turn a cupcake into a hopping good treat.
This sweet little bunny is so fluffy and cute,
you'll just eat it up.

INGREDIENTS

1 cupcake (paper liner removed)
vanilla frosting
sweetened flake coconut
1 large, thin, round
    chocolate cookie
1 jumbo marshmallow
pink decorating sugar
1 large marshmallow
2 mini marshmallows
2 small breath mints
1 pink jellybean
2 chocolate pastels

Tip:
Frosting spreads best when it's kept at room temperature. But cupcakes at room temperature can be soft and fragile. Place cooled cupcakes in a zip-top bag. Then put them in the freezer for about an hour. Freezing makes them firmer, which makes them easier to frost.

1. Stick a fork into the top of the cupcake. Holding the fork in one hand, frost the top, bottom, and sides of the cupcake.

2. Sprinkle coconut over the cupcake until the frosting is completely covered. Remove the fork, and place the cupcake upside down on the chocolate cookie.

3. Hold the jumbo marshmallow so the long sides are up and down. Cut skinny slices off the right and left sides to make bunny ears. One side of each ear will be sticky. Poke toothpicks into the bottoms of the ears. Sprinkle the sticky sides with pink decorating sugar. Poke the ears into the top of the cupcake.

4. Cut the large marshmallow in half. Place the halves at the base of the cupcake as feet.

5. Use a dab of frosting to stick a mini marshmallow in the back as a tail.

6. Cut a mini marshmallow in half. Stick the halves to the face as cheeks. Using frosting as glue, add the mints as teeth and the jellybean as a nose. Finally, add two chocolate pastels as eyes.

Makes 1 bunny

GIFTS FROM the SEA

A day at the beach is full of splashes, sand, and sun. Discover what the waves washed in with this cupcake covered with ocean treasures.

INGREDIENTS
vanilla frosting
1 cupcake
blue food coloring
1 graham cracker
1 piece each of purple, orange,
    red, and green taffy
1 sugar pearl
1 red round fruit candy

~ Piping Tips~
Experiment with different piping tips to get the look you want when decorating with frosting. Round tips are great for outlining details. Basket weave tips can make long, ribbed stripes.

Tip:
Squeeze the taffy between your fingers and in your hands. The warmth of your skin will soften the taffy and make it easy to work with.

1. Frost the cupcake with vanilla frosting. Then mix up blue frosting. Pipe the blue frosting over half of the white frosting, making swirls like waves.

2. With a rolling pin, crush the graham cracker into crumbs. Sprinkle the crumbs on the white half of the cupcake.

3. To make the oyster shell, flatten purple taffy between two sheets of wax paper. With the kitchen shears, cut the taffy into a heart shape. Fold the heart in half to make a shell shape and pinch the pointy end closed. Place a sugar pearl inside the shell.

4. To make the starfish, flatten orange taffy. Cut the orange taffy into a star shape. Mold the cut edges smooth with your fingers.

5. To make the crab, flatten red taffy into a circle. Place the red fruit candy under the center of the circle and press the taffy to it. Snip claw and leg shapes into the taffy around the fruit candy.

6. To make the seaweed, flatten green taffy. Cut grass shapes.

7. Place your ocean treasures on top of the sand side of the cupcake.

Makes 1 cupcake

movie POPCORN TREAT

You can't watch a movie without popcorn. But you also need a treat to satisfy your sweet tooth. No problem! Create the ultimate movie snack with this cupcake covered in candy popcorn.

INGREDIENTS
yellow food coloring
vanilla frosting
1 cupcake
5 white candy melting wafers
crushed ice
water

l. Mix up a batch of pale yellow frosting. Frost the top of the cupcake.

2. To make the candy popcorn, place the melting wafers in a small zip-top bag or disposable piping bag. Leave the bag open and microwave on the defrost setting for 30 seconds. Squeeze the melted candy to one corner. If the wafers are not soft yet, microwave on defrost 30 seconds more. With a kitchen shears, snip off the corner of the bag.

3. Fill a shallow bowl with crushed ice and water. Squeeze dollops of the melted candy into the ice water. They will cool almost instantly into popcorn shapes.

4. Remove the candy popcorn from the water and dry on a paper towel. Then place the popcorn on top of the cupcake.

5. For the movie theater look, cut about 3 inches (7.6 centimeters) off the top of a popcorn bag. Open it up, and place the small bag around your cupcake.

Makes 1 movie treat

Tip:
Melting wafers are solid candy circles that can be melted easily. The melted candy can be used for dipping or molding into new shapes. Each package has directions, so be sure to follow them carefully.

GRINNING GORILLA

It can be a jungle out there. This grinning gorilla will give you a sweet burst of happiness to brighten any day.

INGREDIENTS
chocolate frosting
1 chocolate cupcake
chocolate sprinkles
1 large thin chocolate cookie
2 chocolate-covered cookies
1 chocolate-covered pretzel
2 mini creme-filled
   chocolate cookies
2 brown candy-coated chocolates

1. Frost the cupcake with chocolate frosting. Then cover the frosting with chocolate sprinkles.

2. Place the large, thin cookie in the center of the cupcake.

3. Spread a bit of frosting on the bottoms of the chocolate covered cookies. Stack them on top of the thin cookie to look like a gorilla's face. Top the stack with a pretzel to make the snout.

4. Open the mini chocolate cookies. Use the creme-filled sides for the eyes. Put a dab of frosting on the backs to serve as glue. Then frost on the candy-coated chocolates for eyeballs.

5. On each side of the face, add the other halves of the creme-filled cookies as ears.

Makes 1 gorilla

~ Did you know? ~
Cupcake pans (also known as muffin tins) were called gem pans in the early 1900s.

☮ PEACEFUL
snowman

You may like snowball fights. But the snowmen sure don't! Show the snowman's point of view with this hilarious creation.

INGREDIENTS

vanilla frosting
1 cupcake
white sparkling sugar
1 large marshmallow
5 chocolate melting wafers
1 wafer candy
2 chocolate pastels
1 piece orange taffy
1 red licorice whip
2 starlight mints

Tip:
You can buy piping bags and tips at cake decorating and craft stores. Or you can make your own using a zip-top plastic bag. Scoop frosting into the bag, squeeze out the extra air, and seal it closed. Then squeeze the frosting to one corner. With a scissors, snip a hole in the corner. Cut a small hole for detailed decorations or a wide one to cover large areas.

1. Frost the cupcake with a "cupcake swirl" by piping a circle around the edge. Continue in a spiral shape into the center. Lift the bag at the end to give your frosting a little peak.

2. Sprinkle the frosting with white sparkling sugar.

3. Place the marshmallow on a fork. Holding the fork in one hand, frost the marshmallow until it's covered completely. Then sprinkle the marshmallow with sparkling sugar. Gently take it off the fork and place it on the cupcake.

4. Place the melting wafers in a small zip-top bag. Leave the bag open and microwave on the defrost setting for 30 seconds. Squeeze the melted candy to one corner. If the wafers are not soft yet, microwave on defrost 30 seconds more. With a kitchen shears, snip off the corner of the bag.

5. On a piece of wax paper, pipe the melted chocolate into shapes that look like stick arms. Pipe a peace sign on the wafer candy. Let them dry for at least one hour. Then put them on your snowman.

6. Add two chocolate pastels for eyes. Roll a bit of orange taffy into a nose, and stick it on the marshmallow.

7. To make earmuffs, cut a small length of licorice whip and arch it over the top of the marshmallow. Glue one starlight mint on each side with a dab of frosting.

Makes 1 snowman

sweet TWEET

Explore nature's surprises with this fun dessert. Everyone will be tweeting your praises!

INGREDIENTS

1 cup (240 mL) butterscotch chips
½ cup (120 mL) chow mein noodles
green food coloring
vanilla frosting
1 cupcake
1 piece each of green and orange taffy
1 mini white marshmallow
blue sparkling sugar
3 blue jellybeans

1. Heat the butterscotch chips in the microwave for 30 seconds. Stir. Continue melting at 15-second intervals until all the chips are melted.

2. Stir in the chow mein noodles until well coated with butterscotch.

3. Line a cookie sheet with wax paper. Drop large spoonfuls of the noodle mixture onto the cookie sheet. With the back of the spoon, press a bowl into the middle of each one.

4. Place the nests in the refrigerator for about 15 to 20 minutes.

5. Mix up a batch of green frosting. Pipe leaves of frosting around the edge of the cupcake.

6. Place a nest on the cupcake.

7. Roll a tiny piece of green taffy to look like an inchworm. Place it on the nest.

8. Flatten the orange taffy and cut out a small diamond. Fold the diamond in half to make a beak. Stick the beak to the mini marshmallow with frosting.

9. Brush the marshmallow just above the beak with a bit of water to make it sticky. Use tweezers to place two pieces of blue sparkling sugar on as eyes.

10. Place your chick in the nest. Surround it with three jellybeans to look like unhatched eggs.

Makes 1 full cupcake and 5 extra nests

TIPSY FLOWER TOWER

Celebrate your un-birthday with this tipsy cake. It's so beautifully strange, you'll feel like you stepped into Wonderland.

INGREDIENTS
2 cupcakes
    (paper liners removed)
1 mini cupcake
    (paper liner removed)
vanilla frosting
pink, purple, and green
    food coloring
sugar pearls
2 pieces pink taffy

1. Freeze your cupcakes for about an hour. Then cut the tops off the two large cupcakes on a slant.

2. Spread some frosting on the bottom of one cupcake. Place it on top of the other one. Arrange so that the slanted tops are opposite each other.

3. Spread frosting on the bottom of the mini cupcake, and stick it on top.

4. Push a wooden skewer down through the center of all three layers to hold them together. Then return the cupcakes to the freezer for another 15 to 30 minutes or until firm again.

5. Meanwhile, mix up a batch of pink frosting in a microwave safe bowl. Heat for about 15 seconds in the microwave. Stir. You want the frosting to be a liquid, pourable consistency. Heat another 15 seconds if it is still too thick.

6. Place the cupcake tower on a cooling rack with wax paper below. Spoon the melted frosting over all the cupcakes until they are well coated. When the excess frosting has all dripped off, transfer the tower to a plate. Put it in the refrigerator for 10 to 15 minutes.

7. Mix up a batch of purple frosting. Pipe stripes on the middle cake. With the stripes still wet, place a sugar pearl at the top of each stripe.

8. Mix up a batch of green frosting. Pipe leaf designs on the top and bottom cakes. Add sugar pearls as accents.

9. Flatten one piece of taffy with a rolling pin. Cut it into about five small flower petal shapes. Roll one petal into a tube, and pinch one end closed. Attach the other petals to the pinched end and flair them out to make a rose. Repeat with the second piece of taffy.

10. Attach the roses on the tower with a dab of frosting.

Makes 1 flower tower

GLITZY ARMADILLO

Scaly armadillos get no respect. But this one is ready for the spotlight. Your friends will want a photo of this treat topper ... before they gobble it up!

INGREDIENTS
1 cupcake
chocolate frosting
2 peanut butter sandwich cookies
purple food coloring
vanilla frosting
purple decorating sugar
2 orange circus peanuts

Tip:
If pieces fall off, try sticking toothpicks into the cookie and circus peanut pieces. Then stick the toothpicks in the cupcake.

1. Frost the cupcake with chocolate frosting.

2. Cut both cookies in half. Then on two of the halves, trim off a little more so they are shorter than the other two.

3. Mix up a batch of purple frosting. Pipe a purple edge around each cookie. Then sprinkle the purple frosting with the decorating sugar.

4. Place the two taller cookie pieces in the center of the cupcake. Place the shorter pieces in front of and behind the other two cookies.

5. Cut one of the circus peanuts in half. Mold one half of the candy into a head shape. Snip into the two corners on the top to make two triangles. Fold them up to look like ears. Attach the head in front of the cookies.

6. Pipe two dabs of chocolate frosting on the head for eyes.

7. Cut slices from the other half of the circus peanut to make four legs. Attach two on each side of the cookies.

8. Cut a crescent shape from the second circus peanut for a tail. Attach it behind the cookies.

9. Pipe vanilla frosting on the tips of each leg for claws.

Makes 1 armadillo

SUGAR
BURGER

There's no meat or veggies in this burger. It's just two cupcake buns filled with frosting and candy. Add a side of candy cheese curls, and dessert becomes a meal.

INGREDIENTS

2 yellow cake cupcakes
   (paper liners removed)
chocolate frosting
green and red fruit leather
1 red fruit slice
yellow food coloring
vanilla frosting
1 green gumdrop
2 orange circus peanuts

Tip:
Don't worry too much about how this cupcake looks from the top. It's more important to think about its view from the side. Keep your candies close enough to the edge so they'll be seen when you put on the top bun.

1. Cut the tops off of the cupcakes. Place one top down on a plate.

2. Pipe the chocolate frosting in a circle around the edge. Continue piping in a spiral shape to fill the bottom "bun."

3. For lettuce, cut green fruit leather into thin strips. Place around the edges of the frosting.

4. For tomatoes, cut the red fruit slice into slices. Place on top of the lettuce.

5. Mix up a small batch of yellow frosting. Pipe the frosting over the candy to look like mustard.

6. Spread vanilla frosting on the bottom of the other cupcake bun to look like mayonnaise. Place this bun on top of the stack.

7. For the olive, cut a small hole into the top of the gumdrop. Roll up a small bit of red fruit leather, and stick that in the gumdrop's hole. Poke a toothpick through the gumdrop, and then stick the toothpick into the top of your cupcake.

8. For the cheese curls, cut the circus peanuts in half. Mold each strip into a crescent shape.

Makes 1 burger, 1 olive,
and 4 cheese curls

INGREDIENTS GLOSSARY

wafer candies

candy melting wafers

chocolate covered
pretzels

fruit candy

starlight mints

taffy

fruit
leather

sparkling
sugar

sugar pearls

chocolate sprinkles

decorating
sugar

large, thin
chocolate cookies

peanut butter
sandwich cookies

mini creme-filled
cookies

chocolate-covered
cookies

candy-coated
chocolates

mini, large, and
jumbo marshmallows

licorice twists

circus
peanuts

licorice whips

fruit slices

gumdrops

cream wafer
cookies

pastels

TERMS GLOSSARY

consistency (kuhn-SIS-tuhn-see)—
how thick or thin something is

cream (KREEM)—to mix ingredients
until soft and smooth

dab (DAB)—just a little amount

dollop (DAH-lup)—a small lump or
glob of something

peak (PEEK)—a pointed top

pipe (PIPE)—to make details by
squeezing frosting from a bag

score (SKOR)—to make a straight
line or groove on a flat surface

Read more

Maurer, Tracy Nelson. *Cupcakes, Cookies, and Cakes.* Creative Crafts for Kids. Vero Beach, Fla.: Rourke Pub., 2010.

Rau, Dana Meachen. *Piece of Cake! Decorating Awesome Cakes.* Dessert Designer. Mankato, Minn.: Capstone Press, 2013.

Tuminelly, Nancy. *Cool Cake & Cupcake Food Art: Easy Recipes that Make Food Fun to Eat!* Cool Food Art. Edina, Minn.: ABDO Pub., 2011.

Internet sites

FactHound offers a safe, fun way to find Internet sites related to this book. All of the sites on FactHound have been researched by our staff.

Here's all you do:
Visit *www.facthound.com*
Type in this code: 9781429686174

About the Author

Dana Meachen Rau writes about many topics, including food! When she's not writing, she's being creative in other ways—especially in the kitchen. Sometimes she follows recipes, but other times she experiments with new flavors. And she doesn't need a special occasion to whip up a special dessert for her friends and family in Burlington, Connecticut.

Super-cool stuff! Check out projects, games and lots more at **www.capstonekids.com**